TUMBLING and TRAMPOLINING

796.4 7554
L

**Two Books in One—including
Summary of Trampolining Rules**

By NEWTON C. LOKEN
University of Michigan

ATHLETIC
INSTITUTE
SERIES

STERLING PUBLISHING CO., INC. NEW YORK

Oak Tree Press Co., Ltd.
London & Sydney

ATHLETIC INSTITUTE SERIES

Baseball
Basketball
Girls' Basketball
Girls' Gymnastics
Gymnastics

Junior Tennis
Table Tennis
Tumbling and Trampolining
Wrestling

Seventh Printing, 1974

Combined Edition

© 1970 by The Athletic Institute

"Tumbling" © 1961 by The Athletic Institute

"Trampolining" © 1961 by The Athletic Institute

Published by Sterling Publishing Co., Inc.

419 Park Avenue South, New York 10016

British edition published by Oak Tree Press Co., Ltd., Nassau, Bahamas
Distributed in Australia and New Zealand by Oak Tree Press Co., Ltd.,
P.O. Box J34, Brickfield Hill, Sydney 2000, N.S.W.
Distributed in the United Kingdom and elsewhere in the British Commonwealth
by Ward Lock Ltd., 116 Baker Street, London W 1

Manufactured in the United States of America
All rights reserved

Library of Congress Catalog Card No.: 78-90802

Sterling ISBN 0–8069–4336–X Trade   Oak Tree 7061–2211–9
4337–8 Library

Table of Contents

1. INDIVIDUAL TUMBLING. 5
   The Forward Roll 10
   The Backward Roll. 12
   The Backward Roll from Standing 14
   The Shoulder Roll 15
   The Fish Flop 17
   The Back Extension 19
   The Cartwheel 20
   The One-Arm Cartwheel 22
   Forward Roll in Pike Position 23
   Forward Roll to Wrestler's Bridge 23
   The Head Spring 25
2. INDIVIDUAL BALANCING 28
   The Squat Head Balance 28
   The Squat Hand Balance 31
   The Head Balance 32
   The Head Balance—Arms Folded 34
   The Head and Elbow Balance. 36
   The Forearm Balance 37
   The Forward Roll to Head Balance 38
   The Backward Roll to Head Balance. 40
   The Handstand 41
3. DOUBLES, STUNTS AND MIMETICS 45
   The Chest Balance 45
   The Belly Swan 47
   The Thigh Stand 49
   The Knee and Shoulder Balance 50
   The Foot-to-Hand Balance 51
   The Shoulder Stand on Thighs 53
   The Doubles Roll 54
   The Back-to-Back Toss 55
   The Backward Roll over Back. 56
   The Frog Jump 58
   The Crab Walk 58

The Lame Dog Walk 59
The Elephant Walk. 59
The Seal Walk 60
The Centipede Crawl 60
The Monkey Walk 61
4. INTRODUCTION TO TRAMPOLINING 62
Half Pirouette 70
Full Pirouette 72
Tuck Bounce 73
Pike Bounce 75
5. BEGINNING STUNTS 79
Seat Drop 81
Back Drop 83
Front Drop 86
Knee Drop 88
Half Twist to Back Drop 89
Half Twist to Front Drop 92
Swivel Hips 93
Half Turntable 95
6. ADVANCED TRAMPOLINE STUNTS 101
Front Somersault . . . . - 105
Back Pullover 107
Back Somersault 109
Barani 110
Knee Barani. 111
Front One and One Quarter to Front Drop 114
Full Twisting Back Somersault 117
NATIONAL RULES OF TRAMPOLINING 123
TUMBLING COMPETITION 125
INDEX 127

1. Individual Tumbling

Tumbling is part of a group of activities called gymnastics, designed to promote perfect physical development and fine body control. All gymnastics consist of physical stunts. Tumbling is different, however, because it is performed on mats without any other equipment.

All other activities of gymnastics require special apparatus. One piece of apparatus is a sidehorse.

The parallel bars, another piece of gymnastics apparatus, allow spectacular stunts that require exact coordination. The bars help develop control in body movements.

On the flying trapeze, gymnasts perform graceful and thrilling stunts as they swing through the air to promote a graceful rhythm and develop confidence in their own muscles.

The high bar takes the gymnast further from the floor and allows a wide freedom of movement centered around a single rigid bar.

The trampoline bounces a performer high in the air for a variety of graceful, rhythmic stunts.

Gymnasts often perform in a single stunt more feats of sheer skill and courage than are required of players in other sports during a whole game. The body control and muscular development acquired through gymnastics are helpful to developing skills in other sports.

Tumbling and balancing are fundamental to all gymnastics. For beginning gymnasts, they are the best starting points because they promote muscular development, agility, and body control, yet are relatively safe because they are performed close to the ground. But even in elementary tumbling, don't take safety for granted.

While learning any new stunt, every tumbler should have a spotter, an instructor or fellow student who helps him through the stunt. In illustration below an instructor helps a beginning tumbler through a front head spring.

On more difficult stunts, a safety belt is sometimes used. This is a strong belt with ropes on either side so that the tumbler can flip and turn while two others hold him up safely.

The Forward Roll

This will give you your first sensation of being upside down in tumbling. You have probably done this stunt many times, but let us analyze the correct movement.

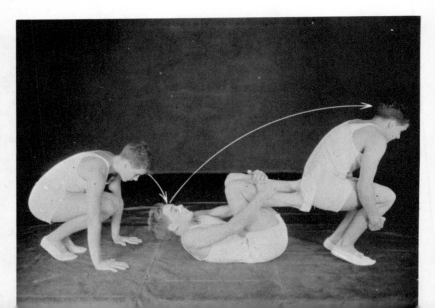

Note the starting position: hands flat on the mat, shoulder width apart, your fingers pointing forward, knees between your arms. From here, push off with your feet and rock forward on your hands.

Just as you feel yourself falling off balance, tuck your head down between your arms. Keep your chin on your chest and put the back of your head on the mat. Keep on rolling, and as the weight comes off your hands and you roll onto your back, grasp your shins and pull yourself up onto your feet. That's all there is to the forward roll.

The Backward Roll

A backward roll is a little more difficult than the forward roll, but it is also more fun, and will give you the feeling of backward movement.

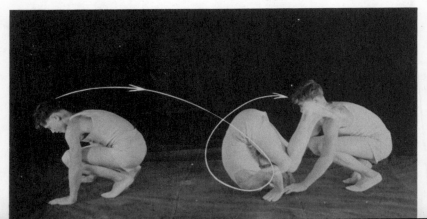

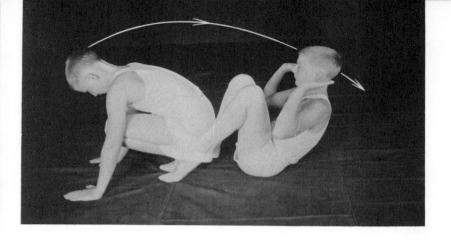

Start in the squat position as in the forward roll. This time push off with your hands. Push quickly, sit down, and start rolling onto your back. At the same time, bring your hands up over your shoulders, palms up, fingers pointing backward. Keep rolling backward with your knees as close as possible to your chest.

As you roll back, your hands will touch the mat at about the same time as the back of your head. This is the crucial motion. You must get ready to push hard with your hands.

Continue to roll over the top of your head and push up off the mat. Keep your knees against your chest until your feet are under you, and stand up.

The Backward Roll from Standing

When the backward roll from squat position feels natural, try it from standing. Just bend your knees and fall backward with your hands back to break your fall. Then continue the roll as before.

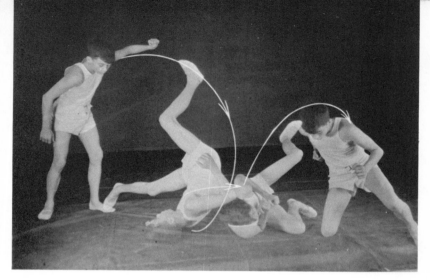

The Shoulder Roll

The shoulder roll is one of the basic movements in many sports. It can be used, for example, to recover a fumble in football, or any time you may fall and have to get back on your feet quickly.

For a shoulder roll to the left, stand with your feet well apart and your left arm extended at shoulder height. Start by throwing your left shoulder toward the mat in a rolling movement. Your forearm and elbow should touch the mat only momentarily.

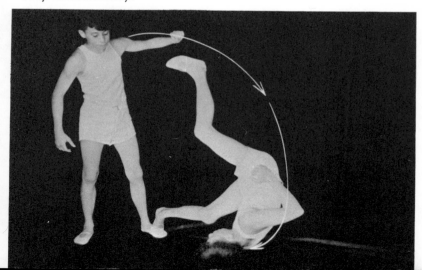

As your weight goes onto your left shoulder, bend your knees and keep on rolling across your shoulders and the upper part of your back.

When you roll over on your right shoulder, keep your knees bent and roll

toward your right knee. Let your weight come on that knee first, and then on your left foot.

Then let the momentum of your roll carry you back up onto your feet. A little practice in this stunt will make you a better player in other sports.

The Fish Flop

Here is a variation of the backward roll called a fish flop. It starts out as a backward roll, but instead of rolling all the way over, straighten out with your feet in the air. Then ease down onto your chest and rock from your abdomen to your thighs.

The essential motion comes just as you are about to push with your hands in the backward roll.

In the fish flop, push harder with your hands and, at the same time, shoot your feet into the air and arch your back. Then, with barely a pause, hold your head back and rock onto your chest, abdomen, and thighs.

As your thighs rest on the mat, push quickly with your hands, bring your feet under your chest—and you are on your feet again.

The Back Extension

A more difficult variation of the backward roll is a back extension from a backward roll.

Carry the backward roll through to the point when you are about to push with your hands.

Then, instead of rolling over, shoot your feet straight up into the air and push yourself up hard with your hands. Kick yourself into a handstand position and hold it momentarily.

Now, bend your knees and arch your back. Then quickly whip your feet out and downward toward the mat and, at the same time, push up with your hands and snap your body into a standing position.

The Cartwheel

The cartwheel stunt makes the tumbler look like a human wheel rolling down the mat with arms and legs for spokes. The important fundamental in this stunt is to keep your body and limbs flat—all in one plane, like a wheel. As you learn it, try to place your hands and feet on an imaginary line down the middle of the mat.

Start the cartwheel with your legs and arms spread. Then, smoothly throw your weight to the left, bending sideways at the hips. Aim your left hand to about 2 feet from your left foot. As your left hand drops, bring your right arm up and over your head and down toward the mat. Your right leg will follow upward.

Just as your right hand touches the mat, push off with your left foot and swing both legs up and over your head in the same plane. Keep up the momentum of the roll and bring your

right foot to the mat about 2 feet from your right hand. Your left foot will swing down as you push off with your right hand to return to the standing position.

The One-Arm Cartwheel

After you have mastered the two-arm cartwheel, try it with one arm. To the left, use your left arm; to the right, use your right arm. It is the same as the two-arm cartwheel, except that you have only three spokes to your wheel instead of four.

Forward Roll in Pike Position

For a forward roll in pike position your body is bent at the hips while your legs are kept straight. This is normally not a stunt by itself, but it is useful as practice for a more difficult stunt to come. Just do a forward roll without bending your knees and end in a sitting position.

Forward Roll to Wrestler's Bridge

Another practice stunt is a forward roll into a wrestler's bridge. Start in a pike position and whip your legs over to a wrestler's bridge—that is, your body arched, supported by your hands, head, and feet.

In the pike position, you should be able to see your knees. Otherwise, you are not in the proper pike position. From there, lean forward until you start to fall off balance. At that point, whip your feet over to the mat, keeping your head and hands in place, and support your body like a bridge.

The Head Spring

If you have mastered all the basic stunts in tumbling and the two practice stunts you just learned, you are ready for the springs. The basic spring is the head spring.

Learn the head spring on a rolled mat at first. This is a more difficult stunt, and a spotter will be necessary until you have mastered the movement.

Start from the pike position as before—forehead on the mat and legs straight. Then lean forward until you feel yourself falling off balance. This is the important step—just as you start to fall forward. From here you must whip your feet out and downward and, at the same time, push up with your hands. As your feet touch the mat, flex your knees and come to a standing position.

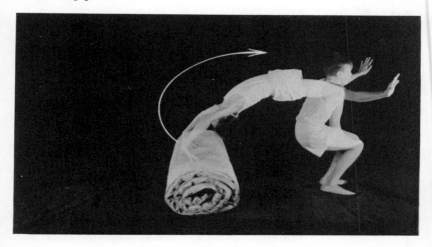

After you have mastered the stunt on the rolled mat, gradually lower the height until you can do the front head spring on a flat mat.

The stunts you have learned so far are basic movements of tumbling. When you are sure of them and they feel easy and natural, you can progress further by combining them into complex stunts that make tumbling exciting fun, as well as a means of developing a finely trained, controlled and agile body.

2. Individual Balancing

Balance is fundamental in body control; it is not necessarily a natural ability. It can be acquired through progressive balancing stunts that are both fun and good exercise.

The Squat Head Balance

This stunt is a simple introduction to balancing, and will get you accustomed to being upside down.

Start from the squat position—your hands on the mat, a shoulder-width apart, and your fingers pointing forward. Your knees should be against your arms above the elbows. From this position, lean forward slowly.

From the beginning squat position, lean forward until your head touches the mat. Then simply lift your toes off the mat. You should feel your weight evenly distributed at the points of the triangle you have made with your head and two hands.

The Squat Hand Balance

Now, as the next step in balancing, try the squat hand balance to help you become accustomed to balancing on only two points.

Start in the squat position with your arms between your legs and your knees above your elbows. Place your hands flat on the mat, a shoulder-width apart, fingers pointing forward.

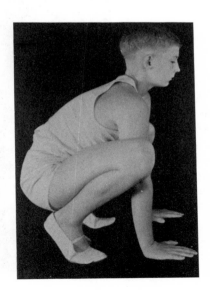

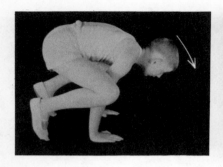 

Lean forward, taking your weight on your hands. Then let your toes lift off the mat until you are balanced on your hands. Here you should keep your head up and press down with your fingers to keep your balance.

The Head Balance

This stunt turns you completely upside down. Make a support triangle with your head and two hands, just as in the squat head balance. Keep your hands only 10 inches from your head and your back arched.

Start from the squat position with your hands pointing forward, shoulder width apart, as in the position on the left. Then put your forehead on the mat about 10 inches from your hands and

walk your feet forward until your hips are high, as in the position on the right. Keep your weight on the forward part of your head.

The next two moves come in quick succession. Keep one foot on the mat and kick upward with the other. Then, quickly follow this kick by pushing off with the other leg toward the upright position.

 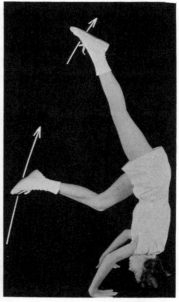

Bring your feet together, arch your back, and freeze at the balance point. Keep your body in the arched position, with your weight distributed evenly on your hands and the forward part of your head. The trick in this stunt is to find the balance point.

To help you find that point, you should work with a spotter. He should catch your ankles as you kick up into this position, and hold them until you feel secure.

The Head Balance—
Arms Folded

In this variation of the head balance, your arms are folded and the support triangle is formed by your head, forearms, and elbows.

34

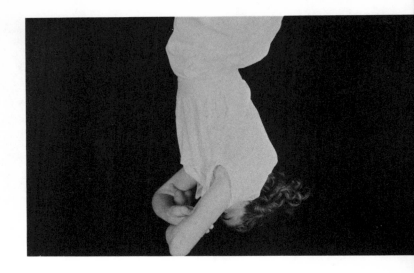

You get into this balance just as you did before. Walk your feet up towards your head, forcing your hips up in the air. Then, kick up with one leg, and follow it with the other leg. Hold the balance, keeping your feet together and your body arched.

The Head and Elbow Balance

This is another variation of the head balance. Place your hands along the side of your head and keep your forearms flat on the mat.

To get up into the head and elbow balance, kick up into position as before, arching your back to hold the balance.

The Forearm Balance

In a forearm balance, your support triangle is formed by your hands and forearms. In this stunt your elbows should be about 12 inches apart and your thumbs touching.

To get into position, get your hips as high as you can with your feet still on the mat. Then kick up to the balance point. Throughout this stunt, keep your head up and your upper arms vertical.

The Forward Roll to Head Balance

Now, combine the forward roll with a head balance. This stunt is a good test of control and balance, and a real achievement when done smoothly.

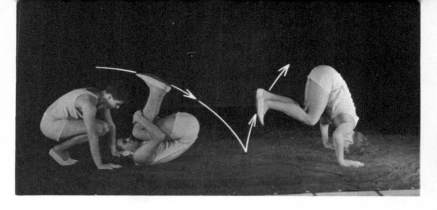

Start the forward roll from either the squat or the standing position. Instead of standing up as you come out of the roll, dive forward and place your head and hands in position for a head balance.

Don't stop the forward roll motion: just dive forward, place your head and hands on the mat and kick up with both feet into the balance position.

The Backward Roll to Head Balance

The backward roll into a head balance is the same as a simple backward roll, until you are ready to roll onto the top of your head.

At this point, continue the momentum of the roll and shoot your feet up into the air. As your weight comes over onto the top of your head, quickly shift your hands back to about 10 inches in front of your head. The quick thrust of your hands stops the backward movement and keeps your body in position.

The Handstand

The handstand is one of the most important balancing stunts in gymnastics. Standing and walking on your hands is not only good fun; it is also a basic part of many advanced stunts in tumbling and apparatus work.

For easier learning, and for safety's sake, you should start this stunt with a spotter to hold your feet. In this way, you can find your balance point and become accustomed to the position. Your back should be arched with your feet together.

Your arms should be almost straight and your hands flat on the mat, fingers spread and pointing forward. Keep your head up and your eyes watching an imaginary line across the finger tips.

In the starting position to get up into the handstand, hands are a shoulder-width apart and firm on the mat. Both feet are

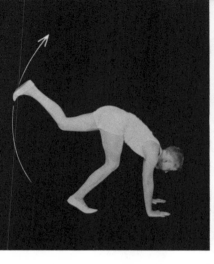 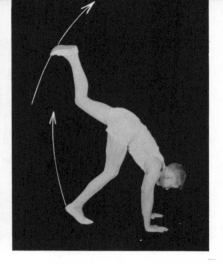

on the mat, one up close to the hands and the other extended back.

From this position kick your back foot up. Then push off with the other foot, allowing the body and legs to go into the upright position.

As your body nears the balance point, bring your feet together, arch your back, and hold the position. If you start to fall forward, you can hold the balance by gripping harder with your fingers, raising your head, and arching your back further. If you start to fall backward, bend your arms.

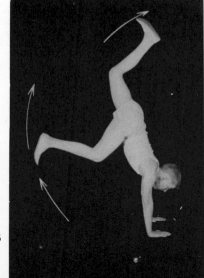 

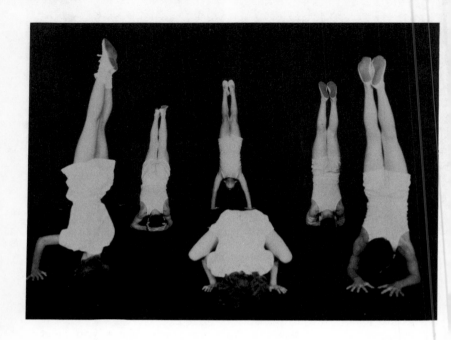

These are the basic balances of all tumbling and balancing stunts. While learning them is good fun, perfecting them brings great personal satisfaction. After you have perfected them, you can combine them with other tumbling stunts to make spectacular maneuvers.

3. Doubles, Stunts and Mimetics

After having learned the basic skills in tumbling and balancing, the sport is even more fun using partners for the stunts.

The Chest Balance

A simple chest balance on one partner's back begins with one partner kneeling on all fours. The other grasps her partner with both hands under the body, and places her chest on the kneeling partner's back.

Then the balancer kicks upward, as in the headstand, holding her chest balance by gripping her arms around her partner's waist and chest.

The Belly Swan

In the belly swan, one partner uses his feet to balance the other.

In the starting position for this stunt, the two partners

grasp hands. The lower partner places his feet on the upper one's hips and abdomen.

Then the top man leans forward while the bottom man lifts him off the mat. Releasing each other's hands, the top man arches his back and holds a free swan, with arms spread, head up, and toes pointed.

The Thigh Stand

In the thigh stand, one partner holds the other on his thighs. At the start of the stunt, the supporting partner puts his head between the other's legs and lifts him onto his shoulders. Then the top partner gets a footing on the other's thighs and leans forward. The bottom man grasps the other's thighs and leans backward, while the top partner spreads his arms and arches his back.

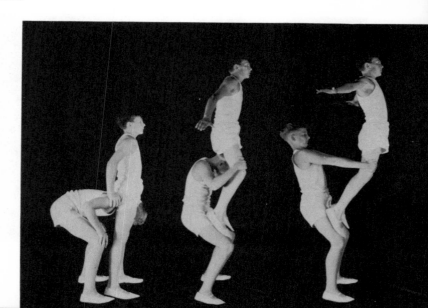

The Knee and Shoulder Balance

In the knee and shoulder balance, the upper partner balances himself on the other's arms and knees. You should not try this stunt without using a spotter until you are sure you can do it safely.

In the starting position, the top man puts his hands on his partner's knees, and his shoulders in his partner's hands.

The upper man kicks up into a shoulder balance with his head almost above his partner's face. To hold the balance, he

arches his back and points his toes. Here it is important that
both partners' arms be straight.

The Foot-to-Hand Balance

This stunt requires complete confidence between partners.
Here too, a spotter is a necessary precaution while you are
learning.

In the starting position, the top man stands on his partner's hands, while the bottom man holds his feet up for the other to hold onto. Then both men push, the bottom one hoisting the other up to arm's length. The top man assists by pushing down on his partner's feet.

After the supporting man straightens his arms, the top man can let go of his feet and balance alone.

The Shoulder Stand on Thighs

The shoulder stand on a partner's thighs is an impressive stunt but requires considerable practice.

In the starting position, the top man's hands are on his partner's ankles while his head is between his partner's legs. The bottom man tucks his feet in under his knees for a maximum of support and lifts his buttocks off the mat. He should keep his arms up to spot the top man in case he falls over.

Then, the top man kicks up. When he has gotten his balance, the bottom man can lower his arms.

The Doubles Roll

In the doubles roll, two tumblers travel up and down the mat in a kind of human loop.

To get started, one partner lies on his back with his feet in the air while the other stands at his head.

While each holds the other's ankles, the top man dives forward in a forward roll and takes the bottom man's feet down with him. The roll brings the bottom man up onto his feet. As he dives forward, the other man is on top again.

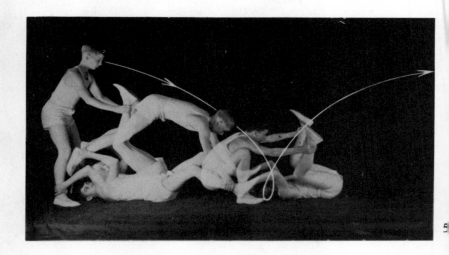

The Back-to-Back Toss

Another doubles stunt is the back-to-back toss in which one tumbler tosses the other over his back.

In the starting position, the partners stand back to back and clasp each other's hands over their shoulders.

Then one partner bends forward, bringing the other up into the air and over his shoulders onto the mat in front of him.

The Backward Roll over Back

Similar to the back-to-back toss is the backward roll over a partner's back.

It starts in the position shown in the illustration. The standing partner will simply roll backward over the other's back.

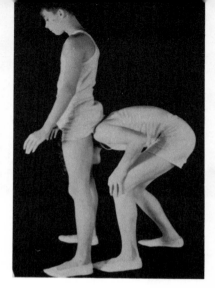

The top man leans back into the roll as his partner straightens up. The roll should be easy and natural as the top man rolls over and lands on his feet. Until you feel confident in this stunt, a spotter should be present to prevent possible injury.

The word "mimetic" means "imitating," and mimetic tumbling imitates the movements of animals. Good for development, these tumbling stunts are still a lot of fun.

The Frog Jump

The frog jump is a stunt that imitates the action of a leaping frog. Start in the squat position, knees outside the arms and hands on the mat. Then leap forward, pushing off with your feet and sailing through the air about 4 feet. Land hands first and bring your feet back up to the starting position, ready for another hop.

The Crab Walk

To walk like a crab, start in a sitting position with your hands behind you and your feet drawn up close. Then lift your

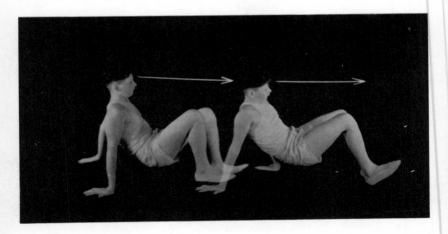

buttocks and walk on your hands and feet either forward or backward.

The Lame Dog Walk

For the lame dog walk, start on all fours. Then lift one leg in the air and run down the mat on one leg and two hands.

The Elephant Walk

You can imitate the lumbering gait of an elephant by walking on all fours with your legs and arms stiff.

The Seal Walk

In the starting position of the seal walk, your arms are straight and your fingers point backward. To imitate a seal, just walk forward on your hands, dragging your legs behind.

The Centipede Crawl

Several tumblers can imitate a centipede in the centipede crawl. Each tumbler straddles the one in front of him with his feet in the other's lap. Then, they travel forward together on their hands and buttocks.

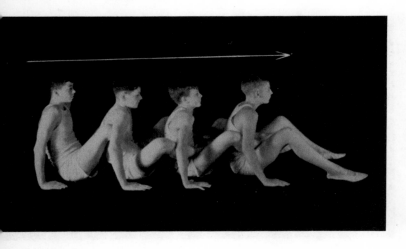

The Monkey Walk

And now the monkey walk. To get into this position, one tumbler lies flat on the mat while the other kneels over him on all fours. The bottom man puts his hands on the small of his partner's back.

Then the bottom man wraps his legs around the other's waist. The top man gets up on his hands and feet, and they are ready to move off in the monkey walk.

4. Introduction to Trampolining

For an activity packed with thrills and excitement, trampolining is hard to beat. A lot like bouncing up and down on an old bed spring as you did when you were younger, trampolining allows you to bounce a lot higher. The increased area of the trampoline gives you more room to perform stunts.

Besides being a lot of fun, trampolining is a great body conditioner. It can help you develop balance, coordination, rhythm, and a keen sense of timing.

The competitive trampoline is a sturdy, table-high metal frame. Stretched within the frame is the performing surface, or bed, about 12 feet long and 8 feet wide. The sheet, made of heavy canvas or woven webbing, is attached to the frame with elastic cords or metal springs.

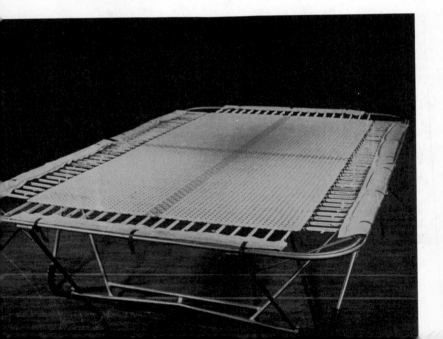

SAFETY PAD

Safety pads should always be on the metal sides of the frame. They are required accessories, protecting you in case you land off the bed.

For further protection, you should have spotters, to catch or warn you if you get too close to the edge.

When you mount the trampoline, always climb carefully onto the bed. Don't risk an injury by trying to leap onto the frame.

Be just as careful when you dismount, climbing over the frame rather than bouncing onto a hard floor. Practice mounting and dismounting a few times to get used to doing it right.

Spend a few minutes bouncing low and easily, to get the feel of the trampoline. As you gain confidence, begin bouncing a little higher.

Hit the canvas with your feet about 18 inches apart. As you land, flex your knees and let your arms come down to your sides.

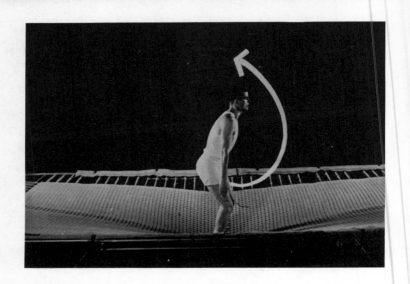

Swing your arms forward and up as you bounce up from the bed. As you go up, bring your feet together and stretch your arms above your head at the top of the bounce. As you drop to the bed again, swing your arms back down to your sides, and open your legs again. If you want to stop bouncing, flex your knees the instant you touch the bed, and hold them flexed. This kills your spring and prevents an uncontrolled bounce.

Work on this simple bounce until the form feels comfortable and natural. Then you can begin trying some of the bounce variations.

The half pirouette is one of the easiest variations to learn. Just bounce, half twist in the air, and come down facing in the opposite direction.

HALF PIROUETTE

Start the half pirouette with a regular bounce. But, instead of swinging both arms above your head, pull your outside arm across your stomach to help you spin. Your outside arm is your right arm if you are turning to the left.

You should find it easy to half-spin your body so that you come down facing in the opposite direction.

FULL
PIROUETTE

By adding a little more twist or spin, you can do the full pirouette. Just pull your outside arm harder across your stomach, so that your body spins all the way around and you come down facing in the same direction as when you started the bounce. To stop your spin as you land, throw your arms to the sides.

Work on both the half pirouette and the full pirouette until you can do them gracefully, keeping your body straight and using the right amount of spin.

Then you can go on to the tuck bounce. Here you bounce high into a tuck or ball, and drop back to the bed in regular bounce position.

TUCK
BOUNCE

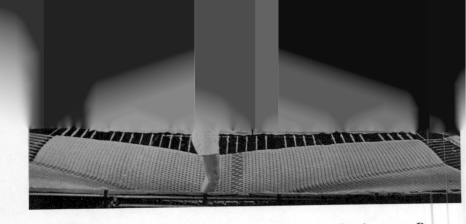

Begin the tuck bounce as you would a regular bounce. But as your feet leave the bed, bring your knees up close to your chest and grab your shins so your body is tucked into a tight ball. On the way down, let go of your shins and straighten

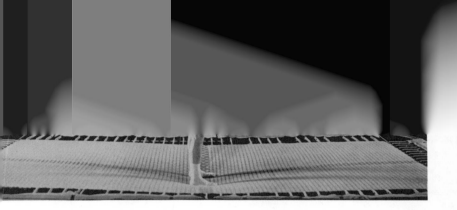

your body so you land in regular standing position. As you land you can either kill your spring or go into another bounce.

Another simple bounce variation is the pike bounce. This is a lot like the tuck bounce, except that you go into a pike or jackknife position instead of tucking into a ball.

PIKE BOUNCE

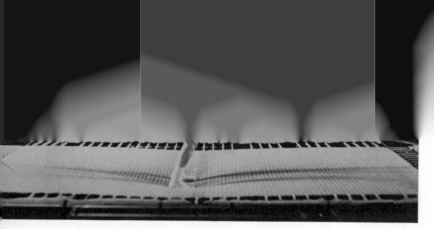

Start the pike bounce with a regular bounce, just as you did with the tuck. Then, as your feet leave the bed, bring your legs up together until they are parallel with the bed. Stretch your arms forward until they touch your ankles. Then straighten out so you land in regular standing position.

76

Once you have learned these elementary bounces, try practicing them in combinations. You might start with several regular bounces, for example, then do a tuck bounce, follow with a pike bounce, and end up with a full pirouette. Don't try

a combination, however, until you have spent plenty of time perfecting each bounce separately.

Your success as a trampoline performer will depend on how well you build one skill upon another. Master each new step through repeated practice. A thorough knowledge of the fundamentals will go a long way toward helping you become a first-rate trampoline man.

5. Beginning Stunts

In a typical gymnastics competition, trampoline performers are required to go through combinations of stunts, called routines. Every performer does two routines.

In each of these routines, you are allowed a maximum of eight contacts with the bed. Judges score the routines on form, continuity, and the difficulty of the stunts.

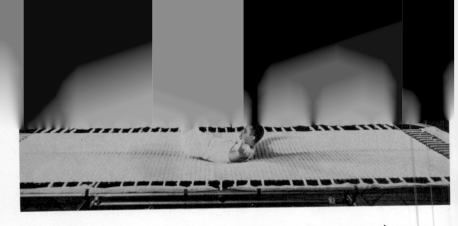

You can use any combination of stunts in your routines, as long as you don't bounce more than eight times. Until you become really expert, however, your best chance of winning is to perform your beginning stunts perfectly.

SEAT
DROP

The seat drop is one of the easiest routines to learn and do well. Just bounce to a sitting position, and then back to your feet.

After a few preliminary bounces, take off as if you were going to do a regular bounce. As you reach the peak of your bounce raise your legs from the hips, keeping your knees straight. Your body should lean backward a little.

Land in a sitting position with your legs outstretched and your hands flat on the bed, a few inches in back of your hips, and your arms slightly bent. After landing in this sitting position, let your bounce carry you back up to your feet, completing the stunt.

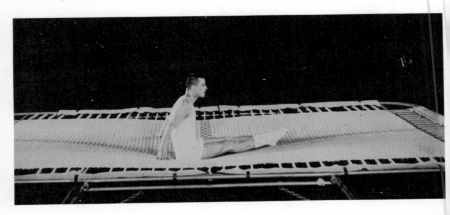

Once you get the feel of the seat drop, you can begin learning the back drop. But before doing it from the regular bounce position, try it first from a standing position. Raise one leg and fall backward to the back drop position.

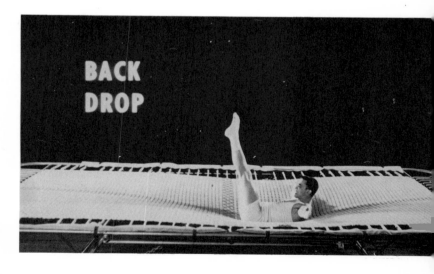

BACK DROP

Then try the back drop from a regular bounce. Let your body fall backward so you come down on your back with your legs stretched in the air. Keep your feet and arms above you. Your chin should be tucked forward on your chest.

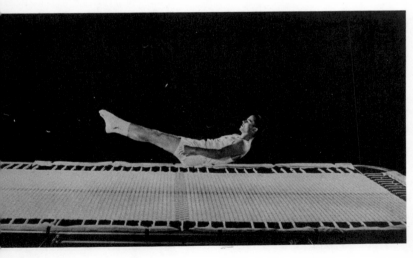

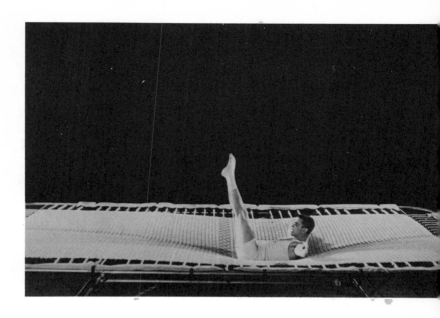

After landing in the back drop position, bounce back to your feet again. Practice the back drop until you can do it perfectly every time.

FRONT
DROP

Now you can go on to the front drop. Begin the front drop with a regular bounce. But turn your body forward so you come down parallel with the bed. Your arms should be out and your

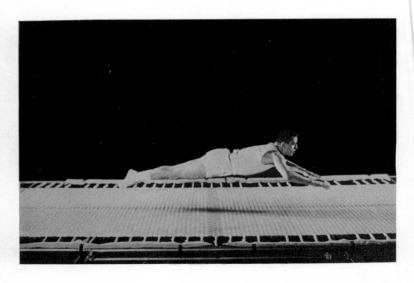

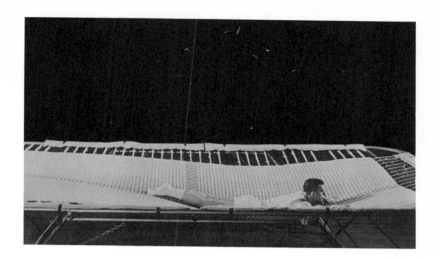

elbows bent slightly to the sides. Land perfectly flat, with your hands, forearms, stomach and thighs all hitting the bed at the same time. Finish by bouncing back to your feet again.

KNEE DROP

Once you master the front drop, you can try the knee drop, as it uses similar form. You perform the knee drop by bouncing to a kneeling position, then springing back to your feet again.

As you come down from a good bounce, bend your knees so that your shins and instep hit the bed at the same time. The weight of your body should be directly above your knees. After

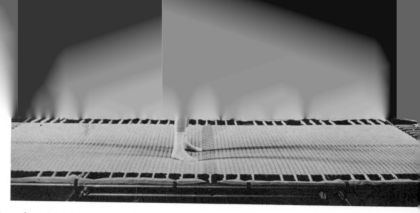

landing in this kneeling position, let your bounce carry you back to your feet.

With a little practice, you'll learn good form in the knee drop, and you can go on to a twisting stunt, the half twist to back drop. In this stunt you start a front drop, then twist in the air so you land in the back drop position.

HALF TWIST TO BACK DROP

After a few preliminary bounces, begin a front drop, letting your body bend forward on the way up. But when you reach the top of your bounce, do a half twist by pulling your outside

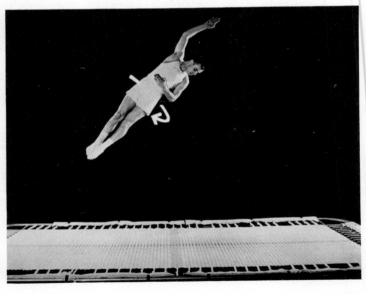

arm across your chest. The twisting technique is similar to that used in the half pirouette.

Your twist should turn you around so you land in back drop position. Then let your spring carry you back to your feet, completing the stunt.

HALF TWIST
TO
FRONT DROP

While you are practicing the half twist to back drop, you can also work on a related stunt, the half twist to front drop. In this stunt, you begin as in a back drop, except that you half twist in the air and land in a front drop.

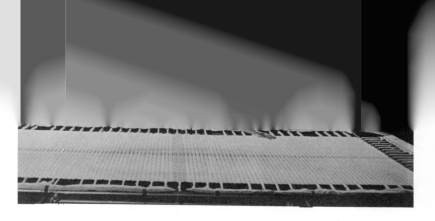

Start your bounce as if going into a back drop. After taking off from the bed, pull backward with your left arm and shoulder and give your body a half twist. Your half twist should spin you forward so that you land in front drop position. Then complete the stunt by bouncing back to your feet again.

Another good beginning stunt is the swivel hips, or seat drop half twist to seat drop. In this stunt you twist from a seat drop to another seat drop facing in the opposite direction. As you

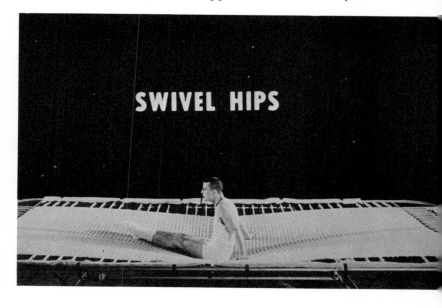

SWIVEL HIPS

bounce off the bed from a seat drop position, twist your head and shoulders to the side, swinging your legs underneath you at the same time. When the twist is completed, you should land in another seat drop facing in the opposite direction. Practice the swivel hips until you can do it smoothly, with your body and legs straight during the twist.

HALF TURNTABLE

Then you can begin working on the half turntable. This stunt is a front drop with a tuck turn to another front drop. Start with a good bounce and land in front drop position with your body hitting the bed evenly, your arms in front of you.

When you bounce back up from the bed, push hard to the side with your hands. As your body begins to turn parallel to

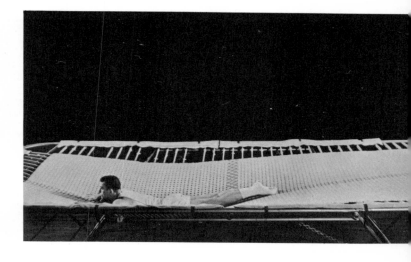

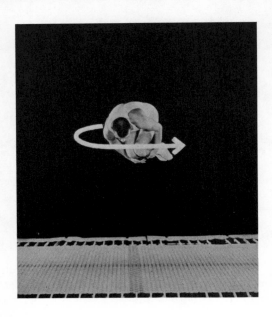

the bed, snap into a tucked position to speed up your turn. As you complete your turn, break the tuck and land in another front drop.

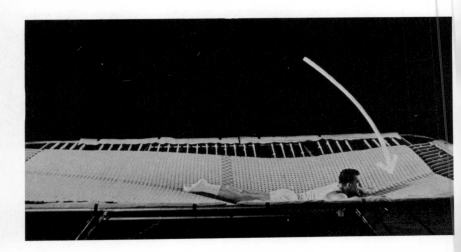

Practice the half turntable and the other beginning stunts until you can do them all well.

Then you can begin putting the stunts together into com-

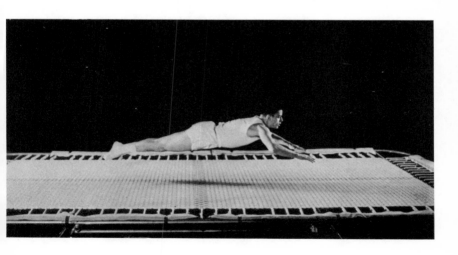

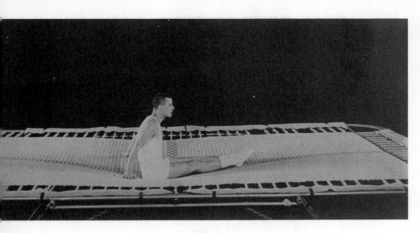

petitive routines. You might start out with a regular standing bounce, for example, and then do a front drop. Bounce up

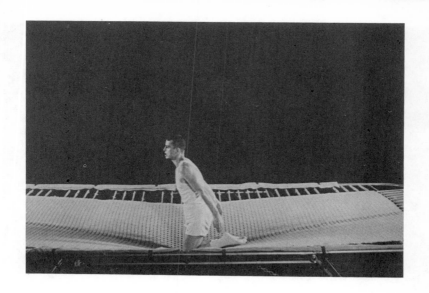

again, land in a seat drop, then a swivel hips, a knee drop, and end up with a half turntable. There are any number of combinations you can put together.

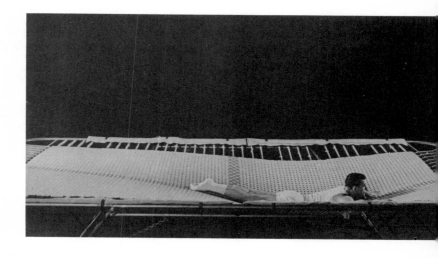

As you gain experience, try to develop your own competitive routines that show off your best form. If you work hard, it won't be too long before your routines are scoring valuable points for your team.

6. Advanced Trampoline Stunts

As your skill in trampolining increases, you will want to add more difficult stunts to your routines—stunts that are more impressive to watch and worth more in the judging.

While you are learning these advanced stunts, protect yourself by using a safety belt. If no belt is available, have a spotter or two guide you through each new advanced stunt. One of the most basic is the front somersault.

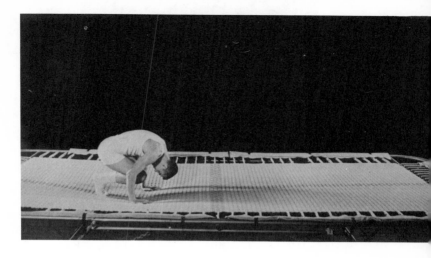

Learn it step by step. Begin with a simple lead-up stunt—a forward roll from a squat stand. Practice it a few times from a still position.

Then go through it from a slight bounce. Gradually add more bounce until you can do the forward roll in the air without letting your hands touch the bed.

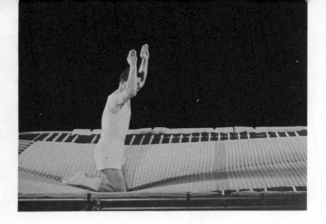

In a while you should be ready to go into a fuller lead-up to the front somersault—the knee drop front somersault to seat drop. From a standing bounce, land in a knee drop.

As you bounce up, flip forward, grabbing your shins while you duck your head. When your legs start to spin underneath you again, pull out of the tuck and land in a seat drop. Work on the timing of your spin until you hit the bed evenly every time. Next, try it landing on your feet.

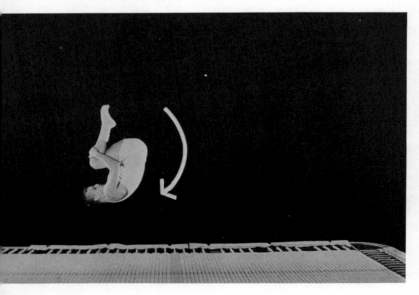

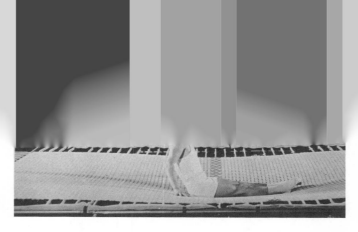

Now you can go on to the complete front somersault from a standing bounce. After bouncing off your feet, try to stay in your spin just a little longer so you will land back on your feet. Start with a regular bounce.

FRONT SOMERSAULT

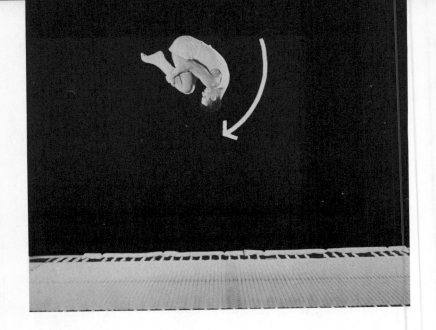

As you come up, grab your shins and go into a tight tuck. Your body spins faster in tuck position, making it easier to complete a somersault.

When your legs are almost under you, pull out of the tuck and land on your feet, flexing your knees to help kill your spin.

BACK
PULLOVER

Always try to land near the same spot from which you started. That's the key to good somersaulting, whether it's forward or backward, as in the back pullover.

A complete stunt in itself, the back pullover is also a good lead-up to the back somersault.

Start the back pullover with a regular bounce, landing on the lower part of your back, with your hands under your thighs.

Coming up from your bounce, pull back hard on your thighs. This starts you into a back pullover somersault that you continue until your feet touch the bed. Then straighten up and land standing.

After you learn the timing for a back pullover, you can try a complete back somersault, adding a little extra bounce so

BACK SOMERSAULT

your spin will carry you all the way around to your feet again.

As you take off from the bed, straighten your body while lifting your arms and keeping your head back.

Then bring your knees up so your hands grasp your shins, pulling you into a tuck position. Spin through your somersault, and when your legs are almost under you again, straighten out and land on your feet. Work on the back somersault until you can safely do it without a spotter or belt.

A little more difficult stunt is the barani. In the barani you start a front somersault, do a half-twist in mid-air, and land on the bed facing in the opposite direction.

BARANI

Before trying a barani from a stand, lead up to it with a knee barani, using your hands. In this stunt, you go from a knee bounce into a half-twist and land on your knees in the opposite direction.

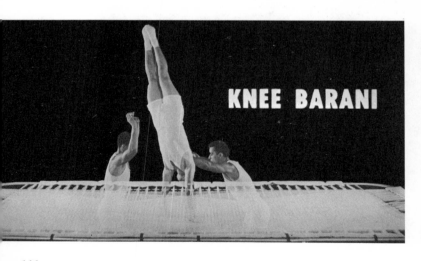

KNEE BARANI

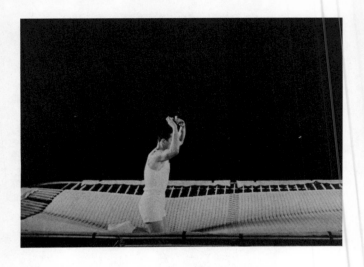

Start it with a knee drop landing. Keep your arms raised overhead, ready to place them on the bed. From the knee landing, bounce forward into a handstand position, kicking

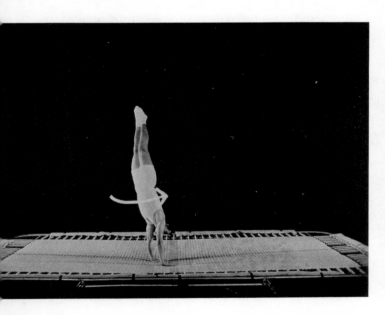

your legs overhead and keeping your arms straight. From the handstand, give yourself a half-twist so your legs carry you on over and you land on your knees again, facing the other way.

BARANI

After practicing it a few more times, you should be able to do the complete knee barani without letting your hands touch the bed. Then the final stunt—doing the barani from your feet and landing on your feet—should come more easily.

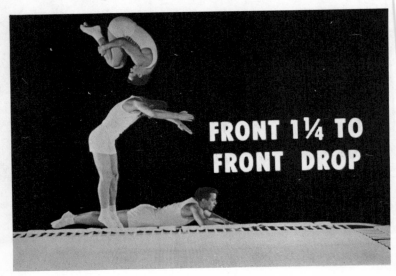

FRONT 1¼ TO FRONT DROP

You can go on to another exciting advanced stunt, the front one and one quarter to a front drop landing. Start out from your regular bounce as if you were going into a regular front somersault.

Grasp your shins into a tight tuck and spin into the somersault. But instead of opening up as if to land on your feet, hold onto the tuck.

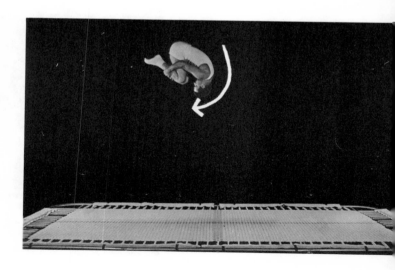

Spin beyond your usual opening point so that you release your tuck a split second later and open up, landing in a front drop position.

Finally, bounce back up to a standing position, and you have smartly completed the front one and one quarter to a front drop.

Next you can work up a stunt that is more difficult yet very exciting—a full twisting back somersault. In this advanced

FULL TWISTING
BACK SOMERSAULT

stunt, you are going to do a back somersault in a layout position, and in the middle of it, execute a full twist or pirouette.

Start as you would in an ordinary back somersault, putting just a bit more lean into it. Raise your arms overhead and spread them apart, ready to provide your twisting action.

After taking off, sweep your twisting arm down. Then quickly bring it up and across your waist towards your chest.

Pull your other arm backward in the direction of the twist and then into a position in front of your chest.

As you twist, try to keep your head turned, looking in the direction you are twisting. Once you have completed the twist, finish by landing on your feet in standing position.

There are many more advanced stunts, none of which can be learned overnight. But by practicing them gradually and regularly, you will find you can become a good trampoline performer and a valuable member of your gymnastics team.

National Rules of Trampolining

Jurisdiction:

The International Trampoline Federation (FIT) makes the trampoline rules for competition throughout the world. The Amateur Athletic Union of the United States (AAU), which is the governing body for all gymnastic sports in this country, is a member of the FIT and is therefore in charge of enforcing the FIT's rules here. Because the AAU is in charge of many gymnastic events, it has formed a National Committee for trampolining, which is entrusted with the development, promotion and general welfare of this sport. Some of the rules of the FIT regarding trampoline competition are listed here, and you should be as familiar with them as you are with performing your routine.

1. ELIGIBILITY: To compete in an AAU trampoline competition, you must be an amateur, and be registered in the district where you live. To compete for a Junior Championship, you must be at least 14 years old, and for a Senior Championship, at least 16 years old. There is no minimum age limit for non-champion competitions.

2. COMPETITIVE ATTIRE: The trampolinist can wear either long pants and footwear (socks and gym shoes, or only socks), or short pants with or without footwear. A shirt must be worn If there is a team, the attire must be uniform for all members of that team, and cannot be changed or modified once the competition has begun.

3. GUARDING OF COMPETITOR: A contestant is allowed to have a spotter stand by during a hazardous part of his routine. The spotter cannot assist the performer, and he should not detract from the value of the performance.

4. REPETITIONS: A contestant in trampoline may never repeat a stunt. However, he may be forced to interrupt his routine because of something which is not his fault, such as a defect in the apparatus. The superior judge or director of the competition can decide if the contestant may then repeat his routine.

5. SCORING: The judges will give each contestant a score after his first routine. The six highest scorers will qualify for the finals and will be required to perform an additional routine. Their final standing will be determined by adding the preliminary score to the score obtained in the finals.

Tumbling Competition

A tumbling competition is conducted in basically the same manner as a trampoline competition. Contestants are required to perform a routine composed of various stunts, and receive points based on the excellence and difficulty of their performances. To achieve the highest score possible, perfect your stunts before entering into competition.

Index

Amateur Athletic Union, 123
Attire during competition, 124
Back drop, 83
 half twist to, 89
Back extension, 19
Back pullover, 107
Back somersault, 109
 full twisting, 117–120
Back-to-back toss, 55
Backward roll, 12
 from standing, 14
 to head balance, 40
 over back, 56
Balance
 backward roll to head, 40
 chest, 45
 foot-to-hand, 51
 forearm, 37
 forward roll to head, 38
 head, 32
 head and elbow, 36
 head, with arms folded, 34
 knee and shoulder, 50
 squat hand, 31
 squat head, 28
Barani, 110–111, 114
 knee, 111–114
Belly swan, 47
Bounce
 pike, 75
 tuck, 73
Cartwheel, 20
 one-arm, 22

Centipede crawl, 60
Chest balance, 45
Crab walk, 58
Doubles roll, 54
Drop
 back, 83
 front, 86
 front one and one quarter to front, 114–117
 half twist to back, 89
 half twist to front, 92
 knee, 88
 seat, 81
Elephant walk, 59
Eligibility for competition, 123
Fish flop, 17
Flying trapeze, 7
Foot-to-hand balance, 51
Forearm balance, 37
Forward roll, 10
 in pike position, 23
 on trampoline, 102–106
 to head balance, 38
 to wrestler's bridge, 23
Front drop, 86
 half twist to, 92
Front one and one quarter to front drop, 114–117
Front somersault, 102–106
Full pirouette, 72
Full twisting back somersault, 117–120
Frog jump, 58
Guarding in international events, 124

Half pirouette, 70
Half turntable, 95
Half twist
    to back drop, 89
    to front drop, 92
Handstand, 41
Head and elbow balance,
    36
Head balance, 32
    from forward roll, 38
    with arms folded, 34
Head spring, 25
High bar, 7
International Trampoline
    Federation, 123
Knee and shoulder balance,
    50
Knee barani, 111–114
Lame dog walk, 59
Mimetics, 57–61
    centipede crawl, 60
    crab walk, 58
    elephant walk, 59
    frog jump, 58
    lame dog walk, 59
    monkey walk, 61
    seal walk, 60
Monkey walk, 61
National rules of
    trampolining, 123–124
One-arm cartwheel, 22
Parallel bars, 6
Pike bounce, 75
Pirouette
    full, 72
    half, 70
Repetitions during
    competition, 124
Rules of trampolining,
    123–124
    attire, 123
    guarding of competitor,
    124

jurisdiction, 123
repetitions, 124
scoring, 124
Safety
    safety belt, 102
    safety pad, 65
    spotter, 9, 65
Scoring in competition, 124
Seal walk, 60
Seat drop, 81
Shoulder roll, 15
Shoulder stand on thighs,
    53
Sidehorse, 6
Somersault
    front, 102–106
    back, 109
    full twisting back,
    117–120
Spotter, 9, 65
Squat hand balance, 31
Squat head balance, 28
Stands
    hand, 41
    shoulder stand on
    thighs, 53
    thigh, 49
Swivel hips, 93
Thigh stand, 49
Trampoline
    construction, 64
    mounting, 66
    rules of competition,
    123–124
    stunts, 70 ff.
Tuck bounce, 73
Tumbling competition, 125
Walk
    crab, 58
    elephant, 59
    lame dog, 59
    seal, 60